I0153028

From

Fear to Freedom

Your Guide to Confident Speaking

By Dr. Dwayne C. Perry

Copyright © 2025
Dr. Dwayne C. Perry
Accelerated Kingdom Development

ISBN: 979-8-9896776-3-4
Library of Congress Control Number: 2025911245

Printed in the United States of America
All rights reserved. No part of this publication may
be reproduced, stored in a retrieval system, or transmit-
ted in any form by any means, including electronic, pho-
tocopy, recording, scanning, or other means, without the
prior written permission of the publisher. The only ex-
ception is brief quotations in printed reviews.

This publication is designed to provide accurate and au-
thoritative information regarding the subject matter covered. The advice and strategies contained herein may
not be suitable for your situation. You should consult
with a professional when appropriate. Neither the publisher nor the author shall be liable for any loss of profit
or any other commercial damages, including but not
limited to special, incidental, consequential, personal, or
other damages.

Cover Design/Editor: NJ Kingdom Enterprises
www.njkingdomenterprises.com

Dedicated to anyone who has ever felt anxious about speaking in front of others or feared that their message would not be heard. You are not alone!

Acknowledgment

As I reflect on my journey from fear to freedom and the discovery of confidence in public speaking, I am deeply thankful for those who have supported me along the way. This book would not have been possible without the encouragement and wisdom from many individuals who have significantly impacted my growth.

Together, we can foster a deeper understanding of our ability to connect with our audience, cultivating an environment where everyone feels valued, empowered, and inspired on their path to becoming confident communicators.

With gratitude,

Dr. Dwayne C. Perry

Table of Contents

Introduction

Their hands were sweaty, their hearts were pounding, and butterflies had taken over their stomachs. Public speaking, although an essential skill for effective ministry and leadership, is one of the most common barriers that aspiring ministers and leaders face, often due to fear. Fear is a powerful and often paralyzing emotion that many of us experience, especially when it comes to public speaking. Whether it is presenting to a room full of colleagues, delivering a toast at a wedding, or sharing our thoughts in a group discussion, the anxiety can feel overwhelming. In my own journey, I vividly remember watching classmates at the front of the room, sweating and voice trembling, while I awaited my turn to speak. These were moments filled with fear, and nearly silenced our desire to communicate.

But through persistent efforts, reflections, and guidance, I have watched transformation into freedom. I discovered that public speaking is not just about delivering words but about connecting with others, sharing ideas, and leaving a lasting impact. In authoring this book, *Transforming Fear into Freedom: Your Guide to Confident Speaking*, I aim to share the insights, strategies, and encouragement that can help you embark on your own journey from fear to confidence.

Countless individuals struggle with speaking anxiety, from students to seasoned professionals. Together, we will unravel the complexities of this fear and learn how to embrace your voice with confidence and authenticity. As we navigate through this journey, you can expect to gain practical tools and techniques that will empower you to overcome your fears, develop your speaking style, and engage with your audience effectively. Each chapter will provide actionable steps, self-reflection exercises, and insights into the psychology of fear and the art of communication. You will learn how to connect deeply with your message, harness your unique strengths, and turn anxiety into a source of energy that fuels your presentations.

More than just techniques, this textbook is about transformation. It is about shifting your mindset, embracing vulnerability, and recognizing that you have a valuable message to share. By the end of our journey, you will not only find your voice but also discover the freedom that comes with expressing it. Let's begin this adventure!

National Statistics on Public Speaking Anxiety

Public speaking anxiety is widespread, affecting a huge portion of the population. According to various studies, these statistics highlight the prevalence of this fear:

National Institute of Mental Health: Approximately 75% of people experience some form of anxiety related to public speaking.[5]

University of California Study: About 20% of individuals experience extreme fear, which can lead to avoidance of speaking opportunities altogether.[6]

American Psychological Association Survey: Over 70% of people fear public speaking more than death, illustrating the depth of this common fear.[1]

This data reflects the challenges many individuals face, underscoring the necessity for an understanding and supportive environment, especially within a seminary context where effective communication is vital.

FAITH OVER FEAR

Chapter 1- The Nature of Fear

Fear is a powerful emotion that can influence our thoughts, behavior, and overall quality of life. When it comes to public speaking, fear often manifests in various ways, causing many individuals to dread the very thought of standing in front of an audience. Understanding the nature of fear, particularly in the context of speaking, is the first step towards overcoming it and unlocking your potential.

Defining Fear and Its Impact on Public Speaking

Fear can be defined as an emotional response to perceived threats or danger. It serves an evolutionary purpose, alerting individuals to potential harm and preparing them to react, often through the "fight or flight" response. In everyday life, fear can be a healthy mechanism that protects us. However, when it comes to public speaking, this same fear can become debilitating.

For many, the fear of speaking in front of others is among the most common phobias. It can lead to a range of responses, including avoidance, anxiety, and self-doubt. The impact of this fear on public speaking is significant: individuals may struggle to articulate their thoughts, lose their place during a presentation, or even avoid speaking opportunities altogether, which can hinder personal and professional growth.

Psychological and Physiological Effects of Fear

Anxiety and Panic:

The anticipation of public speaking can lead to overwhelming anxiety. Individuals may experience racing thoughts, an inability to concentrate, and panic attacks in extreme cases.

Negative Self-Talk:

Fear often breeds self-doubt. Many people begin to question their abilities, leading to phrases like "I can't do this" or "I will embarrass myself." This internal dialogue reinforces the cycle of fear.

Fight or Flight Response:

When faced with the prospect of speaking, the body may react by releasing stress hormones such as adrenaline, which can cause physical symptoms like increased heart rate, sweating, shaking, or feeling faint.

Body Language Changes:

Fear can affect how individuals present themselves. Nervous habits, such as fidgeting or avoiding eye contact, can distract from the message and hinder communication.

The psychological impact of fear can lead to a cycle of avoidance and negative self-perception. Individuals often develop a fixed mindset, believing they are incapable of improving their speaking abilities. Negative thoughts can dominate, overshadowing self-confidence and skewing their perception of their speaking abilities.

Common Triggers of Speaking Anxiety

Fear of Judgment:

One of the most significant factors contributing to speaking anxiety is the fear of being negatively judged by others. Individuals may worry about how they will be perceived, leading to increased pressure.

Previous Negative Experiences:

Past failures or negative speaking experiences can haunt individuals. If someone has struggled with speaking in the past, the memory of that anxiety can trigger similar feelings in the future.

Perfectionism:

Those who set unrealistically high standards for themselves may fear that their performance won't meet those expectations. The desire for perfection can lead to intense pressure and anxiety.

Lack of Preparation:

Feeling unprepared can heighten anxiety and fear. Uncertainty about the content or delivery leads to worry and stumbling during the presentation.

Fear, particularly in the context of public speaking, has profound effects on individuals, impacting their ability to communicate effectively and pursue opportunities. By recognizing the psychological and physiological effects of fear, as well as identifying common triggers, individuals can begin to understand their experiences more clearly. This foundational knowledge is the first step in overcoming fear and transforming it into a source of motivation rather than a barrier. As we continue in this journey, you will learn strategies and insights that will empower you to face your fears and speak confidently.

**MYTHS
VS
FACTS**

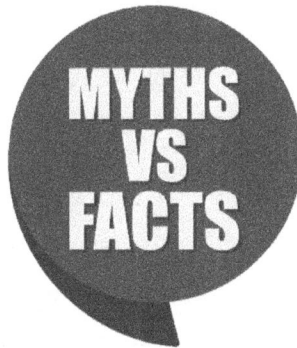

Chapter 2- Myths About Public Speaking

P ublic speaking is often shrouded in misconceptions that can instill fear and constraints on individual potential. Many people shy away from opportunities to speak, believing in myths that overshadow the true essence of effective communication. In this chapter, we'll debunk these common myths and clarify what it really means to communicate successfully, highlighting the key elements that foster effective and meaningful exchanges. By embracing the true principles of communication rather than being hindered by myths, we empower ourselves to connect with others in meaningful ways. Then, our voice becomes a powerful tool.

Myths

You Have to Be Perfect.

One of the most pervasive myths about public speaking is the belief that you must deliver a perfect presentation for it to be effective. The pressure to achieve perfection can paralyze aspiring speakers, causing them to focus more on flawless delivery rather than the message they want to convey.

Communication is inherently human, and mistakes are a natural part of that process. Effective speaking is not about being perfect; it's about being authentic and relatable. Audiences connect more with speakers who show vulnerability and genuine emotion than with those who seem overly rehearsed or robotic. Remember, even the most seasoned speakers make mistakes, and often, it's how they recover from those mistakes that demonstrates their strength and capability.

Only Extroverts Can Be Good Speakers.

Many believe that a dynamic personality is a prerequisite for successful public speaking. The stereotype that only extroverts possess the charisma needed to captivate an audience discourages introverted individuals from pursuing opportunities to speak. While extroverts may naturally enjoy social situations, effective speaking is not limited to personality type. Introverts often possess deep insights and thoughtfulness that can make them incredibly powerful speakers. The key lies in preparation, understanding one's subject, and developing personal style. Great speakers come from all walks of life; what matters most is passion for the topic and willingness to engage with the audience, authentically!

You Must Have Extensive Experience.

Some might think that exceptional speakers are born rather than made, that only those with years of experience can deliver compelling speeches. While experience does contribute to skill, it is not a requisite for success. Every accomplished speaker started somewhere, often with little to no experience. With practice, reflection, and learning from feedback, anyone can become an effective communicator. Embracing opportunities to speak, re-gardless of experience, is the first step toward growth.

Audience Members are Constantly Judging You.

Many people fear that audience members are keenly fo-cused on their every flaw, waiting to criticize or mock them. This fear of judgment can lead to excessive anxiety and stage fright. The audience is usually more sympa-thetic and engaged than you might think. Most people are there to learn, not to judge. Approaching an audience with the mindset that they are there to support you can help alleviate fear and build confidence.

Successful Communication vs. Traditional Notions of Public Speaking

The traditional view of public speaking often paints it as a one-sided, formal presentation characterized by memorized speeches and rigid structures. However, effective communication encompasses much more.

Successful communication focuses on the interaction between the speaker and the audience. Rather than delivering a rigid monologue, consider ways to engage listeners through questions, stories, and discussions that encourage active participation.

Authenticity allows the audience to connect with the speaker on a personal level. Rather than striving for flawless execution, aim to express genuine emotion and passion for the subject matter.

Effective speakers adapt their messages based on audience feedback and reactions. Instead of sticking strictly to a script, be open to improvisation and respond to the energy in the room.

Embrace a growth mindset that views mistakes as opportunities to learn, rather than as failures. Recognize that each speaking opportunity offers a chance to improve skills and understanding.

By debunking common myths about public speaking, we understand that effective communication is not reserved for a select few or dictated by perfection. It is about connection, authenticity, and engagement. As we move forward in transforming fear into freedom, let's redefine our approach to speaking, welcoming each opportunity to learn and grow. Remember, every great speaker was once a beginner, and with the right mindset and preparation, you can thrive in your speaking endeavors.

Chapter 3- Identifying Your Fear

To overcome fear, the first step is to acknowledge its presence in our lives. Understanding what we fear, particularly in the context of public speaking, is essential for moving past these obstacles. In this chapter, we will explore how to recognize and articulate the specific fears associated with speaking in public. Additionally, we'll provide self-assessment tools to help you identify personal challenges and motivations, empowering you to confront and ultimately conquer your fears.

Recognizing and Articulating Your Fears

Fear can often feel overwhelming and nebulous, making it difficult to pinpoint what is causing anxiety. It's important to pause and reflect on the specific fears that arise when faced with the prospect of speaking publicly. Here are some common fears related to public speaking:

Fear of Judgment:

You may be anxious about how others perceive you. Do you worry about being criticized, laughed at, or deemed ineffective by your audience?

Fear of Failure:

The thought of making mistakes, forgetting your words, or not meeting your own expectations can invoke significant anxiety. What specific outcomes are you afraid of?

Fear of Being Unprepared:

The concern that you may not know enough about your topic or that you won't be able to communicate your message effectively can create hesitation. Are there moments in your preparation that make you doubt your readiness?

Fear of Losing Control:

When speaking, the fear of becoming overwhelmed by nerves or emotions may creep in. Do you have concerns about losing your train of thought or appearing flustered?

Encouragement to articulate these fears can lead to a deeper understanding of their origins and triggers. You might consider journaling about your feelings or discussing your fears with a trusted friend or mentor, which can help clarify and express exactly what makes you anxious.

Self-Assessment Tools

To effectively identify and address your fears, consider using the following self-assessment tools and activities.

Task 1: Fear Inventory Worksheet

FEAR INVENTORY
Take inventory of your fear by answering these questions.

1 What specific public speaking fears do you have?

2 What situations bring this fear up for you (e.g., large crowds, unfamiliar audiences)?

3 How does this fear affect your ability to speak? Does it block opportunities?

4 What techniques have you used (or can you use) to manage this fear?

Task 2: Journaling Prompts

REFLECTION TIME

Use the following prompts to guide your reflection:

Respond to the prompts in the space below:

- Describe a time when you felt anxious about speaking. What thoughts ran through your mind?

- What specific qualities do you admire in effective speakers? How can you cultivate those qualities in yourself?

- Reflect on how society views public speaking. Do these societal pressures contribute to your fears? How?

VISUALIZATION EXERCISE

Respond to the prompts in the space below:

Take a few moments to visualize yourself speaking confidently. Imagine the audience responding positively to your message.

Write down how it feels to succeed and how you can make that feeling become a reality.

_____

_____

_____

_____

_____

_____

_____

_____

_____

_____

_____

_____

_____

Task 4: Goal Setting for Overcoming Fear

GOAL SETTING

Write down specific goals you want to achieve related to public speaking. Use the SMART goal framework (Specific, Measurable, Achievable, Relevant, Time-bound) to create actionable steps that will lead you toward overcoming your fears.

Goal Setting

S specific

M measurable

A attainable

R relevant

T time – bound

_____
_____
_____
_____
_____
_____
_____
_____

Identifying your fears is a crucial step in transforming them into opportunities for growth and confidence. By recognizing and articulating what holds you back, you are already on the pathway to overcoming those barriers. Incorporating self-assessment tools will not only give you clarity about your challenges but also motivate you to face them head-on. As you continue on this journey, remember that understanding your fears equips you to break free from their constraints, leading to personal transformation and increased confidence in your speaking abilities.

Additional tools are located in the Appendix

Your
Mindset
Matters

Chapter 4- Shifting Your Mindset

"What we think, we become." Thich Nhat Hanh

In the journey of overcoming the fear of public speaking, one of the most powerful tools at your disposal is your mindset. Specifically, cultivating a growth mindset can transform the way you approach challenges, failures, and learning opportunities. Now we will explore the significance of adopting a growth mindset and provide practical exercises to help you shift your internal dialogue, fostering positive self-talk and visualizing success.

The Importance of a Growth Mindset

A growth mindset, as defined by psychologist Carol Dweck, is the belief that abilities and intelligence can be developed through dedication, hard work, and perseverance. This mindset contrasts with a fixed mindset, which holds that our qualities are static and unchangeable.

Embracing Challenges:

Individuals with a growth mindset view challenges as opportunities to learn rather than threats to their current self-worth. When faced with the prospect of public speaking, they approach it with curiosity and a willingness to improve. By seeing speaking opportunities as chances to grow, you will be less likely to shy away from them.

Learning from Feedback:

A growth mindset encourages openness to constructive criticism. Instead of feeling defeated by negative feedback, individuals see it as an opportunity for growth and skill enhancement. Approach feedback from your peers or coaches with gratitude and use it to refine your speaking skills. It is not an attack!

Persistence in the Face of Setbacks:

Those who embody a growth mindset understand that setbacks are part of the learning process. They do not equate failure with identity but rather view it as a stepping stone toward improvement.

When you stumble during a presentation, remind yourself that every great speaker has faced challenges. Use those experiences as fuel for your growth.

Cultivating Resilience:

A growth mindset fosters resilience, allowing individuals to bounce back from disappointments with renewed determination. Focus on developing resilience so that when you face difficulties in speaking situations, you can quickly recover and keep moving forward.

Exercises to Cultivate a Growth Mindset

Now that we understand the significance of a growth mindset, let's explore some practical exercises to help you embrace this mindset in your speaking journey.

Task 1: Positive Self-Talk

POSITIVE SELF-TALK

To replace negative thoughts with affirming statements that support your journey.

Instructions: Identify common negative thoughts you have about public speaking, such as "I'll embarrass myself" or "I'm not a good speaker."

Write down positive affirmations to counter each negative thought, such as "I am prepared and capable" or "I have a valuable message to share."

Repeat these affirmations daily, especially before speaking engagements, to reinforce a positive mindset.

_____

_____

_____

_____

_____

_____

_____

_____

Task 2: Visualization Techniques

VISUALIZATION TECHNIQUES

To create mental images of success that bolster confidence.

Instructions:

Find a quiet space where you can relax without distractions.

Close your eyes and visualize yourself speaking confidently in front of an audience. Imagine the setting, the people, and feel the energy in the room.

Picture yourself delivering your message with clarity and poise and hear the audience's positive responses.

Spend a few minutes each day practicing this visualization to embed the feeling of confidence and success in your mind.

REWRITE YOUR STORY

To acknowledge past experiences and transform them into growth opportunities.

Instructions:

Reflect on specific speaking experiences that caused fear or anxiety. Write a brief account of each situation.

Next to each experience, write about what you learned from it and how it helped you grow.

By rewriting your narrative, you shift your perspective from one of fear to one of empowerment and growth.

- _____

_____

_____

_____

_____

_____

_____

_____

_____

_____

_____

_____

SETTING GROWTH GOALS

To establish measurable goals that promote continuous learning and improvement.

Write down specific speaking goals, such as "I will give a presentation at my next meeting" or "I will practice in front of friends."

Ensure your goals are SMART (Specific, Measurable, Achievable, Relevant, Time-bound).

Create a timeline for achieving these goals and regularly review your progress and adjust as needed.

Shifting your mindset from fear to growth is a transformative process that empowers you to embrace new opportunities for speaking. By cultivating a growth mindset, you not only enhance your speaking skills but also foster resilience and confidence that will support you in all areas of your life. Remember, every step you take toward positive self-talk and visualization brings you closer to becoming an effective and confident speaker. Embrace the journey and trust in your capacity to grow!

Chapter 5- Building Confidence Through Preparation

We have arrived at a crucial leg of our journey: preparation. The adage "knowledge is power" rings particularly true when it comes to building confidence in your speaking abilities. In this chapter, we will explore practical tips for researching and preparing effective presentations, as well as emphasizing the importance of practice as a key factor in boosting your confidence.

The Importance of Preparation

Preparation is not just about gathering information; it is a systematic approach to creating a compelling presentation. Well-prepared speakers exude confidence because they know their material, understand their audience, and anticipate potential questions or challenges. How is this accomplished? Let's begin with some tips for researching and preparing effective presentations.

Know Your Audience:

Understand who you will be speaking to and tailor your content to meet their needs, interests, and expectations. How? Here are some suggestions.

- Conduct surveys or informal interviews to gather information about your audience's preferences.
- Consider their demographics and what they hope to gain from your message. For example, if you are presenting to industry professionals, include relevant statistics and case studies from their industry to engage them effectively.

Thorough Research and Content Development:

- Gather credible information, statistics, and anecdotes that support your topic. Ensure your content is accurate and relevant.

- Use reputable sources such as academic journals, books, and industry reports.

- Take comprehensive notes and organize your material logically. For practical application, consider creating an outline to ensure your presentation flows smoothly, beginning with an engaging opening, followed by key points, and concluding with a strong takeaway.

Develop Engaging Visual Aids:

- Utilize visual aids (e.g., slides, handouts, videos) to enhance understanding and retention of your content.

- Design slides that are clear, concise, and visually appealing. Avoid cluttering your content with too many words; instead, use images and infographics to effectively support your points.

- Incorporate a story or case study as a visual example on a slide to give your audience a relatable context.

Prepare for Questions and Feedback:

- Anticipate potential questions from your audience and prepare thoughtful responses.
- Create a list of possible questions based on your topic and rehearse how you might address them.
- Practice with a friend who plays the role of the audience, asking them questions to simulate the experience.

The Role of Practice in Boosting Confidence

Rehearse Your Presentation:

- Practice your presentation multiple times to become familiar with the material and timing.

- Rehearse in front of a mirror, record yourself, or practice in front of friends or family. This not only helps with delivery but also reduces anxiety as you become accustomed to speaking.

- Do at least three full run-throughs; this will help solidify your content in your mind and enable smoother delivery.

Focus on Delivery Techniques:

- Pay attention to your vocal tone, body language, and eye contact during practice.

- Work on varying your vocal inflection to emphasize key points, maintaining good posture, and using gestures to reinforce your message.

- During practice, consciously maintain eye contact with the audience members (or imaginary ones) to establish a connection. What you practice will become ingrained.

Simulate the Real Experience:

- Rehearse in an environment where you will be speaking to get comfortable with the space.
- If possible, visit the venue ahead of time to practice standing, moving, and using any available technology.
- Practice navigating any equipment or presentation tools to ensure there are no surprises on the day.

Utilize Positive Affirmations:

- Incorporate positive affirmations into your preparation routine to build your self-confidence.
- Develop specific statements that resonate with your goals, such as "I am well-prepared and confident" or " I have a valuable message to share."

- Repeat these affirmations while you practice to reinforce a positive mindset before the actual presentation.

Building confidence through preparation is essential for overcoming the fear of public speaking. By understanding your audience, conducting thorough research, creating engaging materials, and practicing regularly, you equip yourself with the tools to deliver a compelling presentation. Remember that confidence comes not only from knowledge but from the familiarity and comfort you create through thorough preparation. As you invest the time into preparing, you will find yourself more at ease, poised, and ready to share your message with impact.

Chapter 6- Techniques for Managing Anxiety

It feels like butterflies in your stomach! Fear and anxiety are two of the most significant barriers to effective public speaking. Many individuals feel a heightened sense of pressure and nervousness just before taking the stage or addressing an audience. However, with the right techniques in place, you can learn to manage this anxiety effectively. Let's explore several relaxation techniques and coping mechanisms to help you handle anxiety before and during a speaking event, allowing you to present with confidence and clarity.

Understanding the Impact of Anxiety:

Before diving into specific techniques, it's essential to recognize that experiencing anxiety is a normal response. Understand that many speakers, even seasoned professionals, wrestle with nervousness. The key is managing the anxiety in a way that does not hinder your ability to communicate effectively. By implementing relaxation techniques, you can calm your nerves and shift your focus away from fear.

Deep Breathing:

Deep breathing helps activate the body's relaxation response and can significantly reduce feelings of anxiety. Here is how to practice this technique. Find a quiet space before your speaking engagement. Close your eyes and inhale slowly through your nose for a count of four, allowing your abdomen to expand. Hold your breath for a count of four. Exhale slowly through your mouth for a count of six or eight. Repeat this process for a few minutes until you feel calmer and more centered.

Use deep breathing right before stepping onto the stage to help ground yourself and alleviate tension.

Mindfulness:

Mindfulness involves being fully present and aware of your thoughts and feelings without judgment. It can help reduce anxiety and increase focus. Here are tips for practicing this technique. Take a few moments before your presentation to focus on the present moment. Acknowledge your feelings of anxiety, but don't let them control you. Tune into your surroundings: notice the sounds, sights, and smells in the environment. Practice grounding exercises by feeling your feet on the floor or focusing on the sensation of your breath.

Incorporate mindfulness techniques during your preparations to remain calm and focused, especially when nerves begin to rise.

Visualization:

Visualization is a powerful mental technique that allows you to imagine success and build confidence before your presentation. Practicing this technique is simple as well. Find a quiet space where you can relax. Close your eyes and create a vivid mental image of yourself delivering a successful speech to your audience. Picture the audience engaged, responsive, and supportive.

Imagine yourself feeling calm, collected, and delivering your message with clarity and enthusiasm. Visualize the positive outcomes of your presentation, including audience applause and appreciation. Spend a few minutes each day visualizing your success in public speaking, particularly in the lead-up to an event. This will undoubtedly help solidify your self-confidence.

Coping Mechanisms for Speaking Anxiety

Pre-Speaking Rituals:

Establish a personal pre-speaking ritual to help ease anxiety. This could include a specific routine you follow before each presentation, such as a prayer, affirmation, or stretching exercise.

Pre-speaking rituals create a sense of familiarity and comfort, signaling your brain that you are ready to perform.

Positive Affirmations:

Use positive affirmations to counter any negative thoughts and reinforce a positive mindset. Here are few examples that you may choose to use:

- "I am well-prepared and capable."
- "My message is valuable and will resonate with my audience."
- "I embrace this opportunity to share my thoughts with confidence."

As part of your preparation, repeat these affirmations to yourself in the mirror or write them down in a notebook.

Engaging with the Audience:

Shift your focus from your anxiety to the audience. Remember that they are there to hear your message and support you. They came to hear you... so speak to them!
Make eye contact, smile, and engage with the audience before starting your speech. This connection can help create a more positive atmosphere.

Practice Makes Perfect:

The more you practice, the more familiar the material becomes. Thorough rehearsal helps alleviate anxiety by increasing confidence in your content and delivery.

Managing speaking anxiety is essential for transforming fear into confidence. By incorporating relaxation techniques such as deep breathing, mindfulness, and visualization, you can create a sense of calmness that allows you to focus on your message. Additionally, employing coping mechanisms such as pre-speaking rituals, positive affirmations, and audience engagement will empower you to navigate anxiety effectively. Embrace these strategies as tools for success, enabling you to present with assurance and clarity. Each step you take toward mastering your fear will pave the way for a more confident and impactful speaking experience.

Chapter 7- Knowing Your Audience

We touched on this topic in a previous chapter. However, because it is so essential, it warrants a deeper dive. In the art of public speaking, one of the most critical factors influencing the effectiveness of your message is your audience. Understanding who your audience is allows you to tailor your delivery and content in ways that resonate with them, ensuring that your message is not only heard but also felt. In this chapter, we will discuss the importance of knowing your audience and provide practical tips for engaging and connecting with different types of listeners.

The Importance of Understanding Your Audience

Tailoring Your Message:

Knowing your audience enables you to adjust your speech according to their interests, values, and needs. By understanding what matters to them, you can create relevance and provide insights that directly address their concerns or aspirations.

For example, when speaking to young professionals about career development, you might include contemporary examples and practical advice that aligns with their stage of life, making your message more impactful.

Building Rapport and Connection:

Understanding your audience helps establish a foundation for rapport, allowing you to connect on a personal level. When people feel seen and understood, they are more inclined to listen and engage with your message. When you understand your audience, you can incorporate anecdotes or humor that resonate with their experiences, making them feel more engaged in your presentation.

Anticipating Questions and Concerns:

A thorough understanding of your audience allows you to anticipate questions or objections they may have regarding your topic. This foresight enables you to prepare responses and address potential concerns proactively during your presentation. For example, if you know your audience is skeptical about a new approach, you can present data or case studies that counter their objections directly.

Enhancing Engagement and Participation:

By recognizing the dynamics of your audience, you can incorporate elements that encourage participation, such as questions, discussions, or interactive features. Engaged audiences are more likely to retain information and stay focused. According to Freeman et al, engagement strategies have been shown to increase information retention by up to 60% (2014)

Tips for Engaging and Connecting with Different Types of Audiences

Conduct Audience Research:

Before your presentation, take the time to learn about your audience's demographics, interests, and any prior knowledge they may have of the topic. This can be done through surveys, social media, or informal conversations. Use this information to shape your content and examples, ensuring relevance and connection.

Adapt Your Language and Tone:

Consider the vocabulary, jargon, and tone that will resonate with your audience. For instance, when speaking to academics, you may use more technical language, while a general audience might prefer simpler terms. A key to maintaining engagement is to strive for clarity and alignment with your audience's level of understanding.

Use Stories and Relatable Examples:

Be intentional about incorporating anecdotes and examples that your audience can relate to. Personal stories make your message memorable and help establish a deeper connection. Tailor your stories to reflect the background and interests of your audience. For example, a youth group might appreciate a story about overcoming challenges during adolescence.

Encourage Interaction and Feedback:

Create opportunities for your audience to engage during your presentation. This could include asking open-ended questions, conducting polls, or facilitating small group discussions. Allow for moments of interaction to clarify points and invite audience contributions. Be responsive to their input, which can enhance the overall experience.

Read the Room:

Pay attention to your audience's non-verbal cues. Are they nodding, smiling, or showing signs of disengagement? Adjust your presentation accordingly based on their reactions. If you notice the audience is losing interest, consider shifting your approach, perhaps by changing your tone, involving them with a question, or emphasizing a point that seems to resonate.

Knowing your audience is a crucial skill in public speaking that transforms the impact of your message. By tailoring your content, building rapport, anticipating concerns, and engaging your listeners, you can create a memorable presentation. As you practice these techniques, remember that each audience is unique, and understanding their dynamics will enhance not only your confidence but also their connection to your message. A well-prepared speaker who knows their audience is poised to leave a lasting impression and inspire positive action.

Chapter 8- Vocal and Physical Presence

The way you present yourself physically and vocally plays a crucial role in effective public speaking. Your voice and body language are powerful tools in conveying your message and engaging your audience. In this chapter, we will teach techniques to improve voice projection, tone, and body language, while also exploring how non-verbal communication influences audience perception.

Improving Voice Projection and Tone

Voice Projection:

Voice projection is the ability to speak loudly enough to be heard clearly without straining your vocal cords. It helps convey confidence and authority. Here are some exercises to help improve yours.

- Start with diaphragmatic breathing. Stand or sit up straight, take a deep breath in through your nose, allowing your abdomen to expand. Exhale slowly through your mouth. Practicing this can help you control your breath and support your voice.

- Practice projecting your voice by reading a passage aloud in a clear and strong voice. Imagine you are speaking to someone at the back of the room. Focus on articulating each word without shouting, and gradually increase the volume.

Tone Variation

The tone of your voice conveys emotion and can significantly impact the reception of your message. A varied tone can maintain audience interest and emphasize key points, while a monotone can quickly put them to sleep.

- Experiment with your pitch while reading aloud. Try going higher or lower at different parts of your message to express excitement, seriousness, or emotion.

- Incorporate pauses to make important points stand out. This will enable your words to have a greater impact and allow the audience time to fully absorb your message.

Enhancing Body Language

Eye Contact:

Maintaining eye contact establishes a connection with your audience and builds trust. It shows that you value their presence and are engaged in the conversation.

Practice looking at various sections of the audience (right, center, left) rather than focusing on a single spot. Aim to sustain eye contact for several seconds with different individuals. That personal connection draws them in.

Gestures:

Hand gestures can help emphasize key points and enhance the delivery of your message. They make your presentation more dynamic and engaging. Use natural gestures that feel comfortable to you. Avoid overdoing it; instead, practice gestures that complement your speech, rather than distracting from it. Rehearse your speech while integrating gestures to reinforce your points.

Posture and Positioning:

Your posture communicates confidence and authority. An open and relaxed posture encourages the audience to be receptive to your message. Stand or sit up straight with your shoulders back. Avoid crossing your arms, which can signal defensiveness. Move with purpose around the speaking area, which can create engagement and interest.

Facial Expressions:

Facial expressions convey emotions and reinforce the message you are communicating. A warm smile can make the audience feel welcome and at ease. Be aware of your facial expressions while speaking. Use expressions that reflect the tone of your message, such as smiling when sharing positive stories and adopting a serious face when discussing important topics.

The Role of Non-Verbal Communication

Understanding Non-Verbal Cues:

Non-verbal communication includes body language, facial expressions, tone of voice, and gestures. Together, these cues can convey more meaning than words alone. Research indicates that non-verbal cues contribute significantly to how messages are interpreted; some studies have shown that up to 93% of communication is non-verbal (Mehrabian, 1971).

Impact on Audience Perception

Positive non-verbal communication, such as open gestures and engaging eye contact, fosters a strong connection with the audience, encouraging active listening and participation. Confident posture and vocal projection enhance speaker credibility, helping establish trust with the audience. Conversely, negative body language can lead to disengagement and doubt.

Aligning Verbal and Non-Verbal Communication:

Ensure that your non-verbal cues align with your verbal message. For example, if you are sharing a serious message, your body language should reflect that seriousness. Actively observe the audience's reactions to your nonverbal cues and adjust your delivery accordingly. This awareness helps create an interactive environment.

Mastering vocal and physical presence is essential for becoming an effective speaker. By refining your voice projection, tone, and body language, you can enhance your ability to connect with your audience and deliver your message with greater confidence. Understanding the vital role of non-verbal communication further solidifies your presence as a speaker. As you practice these techniques, remember that authenticity is key; be true to yourself and let your personality shine through your delivery. By doing so, you will create an engaging and memorable experience for your audience, making an impact that resonates long after you leave the stage.

Chapter 9- Low-Stakes Speaking Opportunities

As you embark on your journey to becoming a more confident speaker, engaging in low-stakes speaking opportunities can play a crucial role in building your skills and self-assurance. These informal settings provide a supportive environment to practice without the pressure that often accompanies formal presentations. Would you like to know how to seek out these opportunities and use them to enhance your speaking skills in comfortable contexts? Let's explore.

The Importance of Low-Stakes Speaking

Building Confidence Gradually:

Low-stakes opportunities allow you to practice speaking in a less intimidating format, helping you to gradually build your confidence. By starting small, you can slowly cultivate your skills without the fear of immediate judgment or significant consequences. As you gain confidence in these smaller settings, you will be better prepared for larger audiences and more formal situations.

Experimenting with Content and Style:

Informal speaking environments provide an opportunity to experiment with various content and delivery styles. You can try new techniques, jokes, or anecdotes that you might hesitate to use in formal presentations. This helps you discover what resonates with your audience and what communication style feels most comfortable for you.

Receiving Immediate Feedback:

In casual settings, you can receive real-time feedback from friends, family, or small groups. This feedback is invaluable for improving your skills and understanding how your message is received. Constructive feedback helps refine your delivery and content, enabling you to make adjustments that lead to more effective speaking.

Ideas for Practicing in Supportive Environments

Participate in Small Group Discussions:

Engage in small-group settings, such as Bible studies, book clubs, or community meetings. These gatherings often allow personal sharing and discussions. To optimize the practice, volunteer to lead discussions or share insights, using these opportunities to practice articulating your thoughts clearly and effectively.

Host Informal Gatherings:

Organize small gatherings with friends or family where you can share a topic of interest or lead a light-hearted discussion. Use this chance to practice speaking while fostering a relaxed atmosphere, allowing for authentic engagement and connection.

Utilize Online Platforms:

Join virtual meetups or forums where you can speak on topics that interest you in front of a small audience.

Platforms like Zoom or social media groups offer great opportunities for this type of engagement. Set up a casual online session where you can present a topic and encourage discussion afterward, helping to ease any fear of speaking in larger formats.

Volunteer for Speaking Engagements:

Look for opportunities to speak at local events, community service organizations, or schools. They can sometimes need speakers for panel discussions, workshops, or motivational talks. Start with smaller events or gatherings, where the audience is more familiar and supportive. This can help build your credibility and speaking experience gradually. Put in the reps!

Practice with Family and Friends:

Use gatherings with family or friends as practice sessions. You can ask them for feedback or even conduct mini-presentations on topics you're passionate about. Create a fun and supportive environment where family members can provide encouragement and constructive criticism.

Low-stakes speaking opportunities are essential stepping stones in your journey toward confident public speaking. By engaging in informal settings, experimenting with your delivery, and gradually building your skills, you lay a strong foundation for success in more significant speaking situations. Remember, every opportunity, no matter how small, contributes to your growth as a speaker. Embrace these moments, and allow them to empower you as you work toward mastering the art of communication.

WE WANT YOUR
FEEDBACK

Chapter 10- Getting Feedback and Adjusting

Feedback is a crucial component of growth in any skill, and when it comes to public speaking, it holds transformative power. Now we will explore the importance of constructive feedback, how to solicit it effectively, and teach you how to analyze and make necessary adjustments to improve your speaking abilities.

The Importance of Constructive Feedback

A Catalyst for Improvement:

Constructive feedback provides insights that help you identify your strengths and weaknesses. It enables you to identify areas that may require improvement, which is crucial for ongoing development. Feedback helps bridge the gap between your current abilities and where you aspire to be. Understanding what worked well and what didn't can guide your future efforts.

Encouraging Reflection:

Feedback encourages self-reflection and critical thinking. When you seek out input, you engage in a process of evaluating your performance, which fosters deeper learning. After delivering a presentation, reflecting on the feedback received prompts you to consider how well the audience engaged and what might enhance future presentations.

Building Confidence:

Regular feedback helps to normalize the learning process. When you see feedback as an opportunity rather than criticism, it builds your confidence as you witness your growth over time. Recognizing that feedback is an integral part of the journey toward mastery enables you to embrace it without fear.

How to Solicit Feedback Effectively

Be Specific in Your Request:

When asking for feedback, be clear about what aspects you want input on, such as delivery, content, engagement, or clarity. Instead of saying, "What did you think?" you might ask, "How well did I engage the audience during this part of the speech?"

Choose Trusted Individuals:

Seek feedback from those who understand your objectives and can provide honest, constructive criticism. This could include mentors, peers, or even members of your audience. Look for people who will be supportive but also challenge you to improve.

Create an Open Atmosphere:

Encourage an environment where feedback can be delivered openly and comfortably. Ensure that those you ask know their honest opinions are valued and that the goal is your growth. Help them feel free to be honest.

Utilize Feedback Forms or Surveys:

Consider creating anonymous feedback forms or surveys to allow listeners to provide their thoughts without hesitation. Prepare questions that focus on different aspects of your presentation and encourage thoughtful responses.

Review and Reflect on Feedback:

After receiving feedback, take time to review it thoroughly. Analyze it. Look for patterns in the responses, noting comments you receive multiple times. Consider creating a feedback journal where you can document what you received and your thoughts on how it aligns with your own self-assessment.

Identify Actionable Points:

Distill feedback into specific, actionable items. Rather than being overwhelmed by general comments, break down responses into clear steps for improvement. If feedback indicates that your pacing was too fast, plan to rehearse at a slower tempo next time.

Set Goals for Improvement:

Based on the analysis of feedback, set realistic goals for your next speaking opportunity. Establish clear objectives for what you want to improve.

Use **SMART** goals (Specific, Measurable, Achievable, Relevant, Time-bound) to ensure your goals are effective.

Practice and Implement Changes:

Finally, incorporate the feedback by practicing the adjustments you've identified. Rehearse with an emphasis on the areas that need improvement, applying the lessons learned from the feedback. Consider conducting a practice presentation in front of a trusted peer or mentor and ask for immediate feedback to evaluate your progress.

Getting feedback and adjusting accordingly is a vital part of the growth process in public speaking. By soliciting feedback, analyzing it thoughtfully, and making the necessary adjustments, you take significant steps toward becoming an impactful and confident speaker. Remember that every piece of feedback is a chance to learn and grow, turning each speaking opportunity into a steppingstone.

Chapter 11- Handling Difficult Situations

Public speaking can be an exhilarating experience, but it can also present unique challenges that may throw even the most seasoned speakers off balance. The ability to handle difficult situations is a crucial skill that can make the difference between a successful presentation and a stressful experience. Therefore, it is important to be prepared for potential challenges, like technical difficulties and disruptive audience members. Let's review strategies for maintaining composure and professionalism when faced with adversity.

Preparing for Potential Challenges

Technical Difficulties:

Whether it's a malfunctioning microphone, presentation slides that won't load, or audio issues, technical difficulties can occur at any time. Understanding that these issues can arise helps reduce anxiety about the unexpected. Rather than viewing technical problems as catastrophic failures, see them as opportunities for problem-solving. Keeping a calm and collected attitude is essential for managing the situation effectively.

Disruptive Audience Members:

Audience disruptions can include side conversations, late arrivals, or even hecklers. Recognizing these common scenarios can prepare you emotionally and mentally. Anticipating potential disruptions can reduce fear and allow you to focus on solutions rather than the anxiety of being disrupted. People will be people, but you are in control!

Environmental Factors:

Noise from outside, unexpected interruptions, or an uncomfortable venue can also affect your performance. Be prepared to adapt your presentation to minimize the effects of these distractions, such as resetting focus or adjusting your volume.

Strategies for Maintaining Composure and Professionalism

Stay Calm and Collected:

Practice deep breathing exercises before your presentation. If anxiety arises, pause and take a slow, deep breath to help calm your nerves and regain focus. Additionally, use grounding techniques, such as feeling your feet on the floor or focusing on a specific object in the room, to help anchor yourself when you feel overwhelmed.

Acknowledge and Address Technical Issues:

If a technical difficulty arises, address it calmly. For instance, if the projector doesn't work, acknowledge the issue with a simple statement like, "It seems we're having a bit of technical difficulty, but let's move on to the next point while we get this sorted." While troubleshooting, keep the audience engaged by asking a question related to your topic or sharing a relevant anecdote, turning the moment into an opportunity for connection.

Handling Disruptive Audience Members:

If someone is being disruptive, remain composed and professional. You might say, "I appreciate your enthusiasm, but let's keep the focus on this discussion." This demonstrates respect while redirecting the attention. If disruptions continue, calmly state that you will be available for questions after the presentation to maintain control and respect.

Reframe Your Perspective on Anxiety:

Reframe nervousness into excitement. Remind yourself that the adrenaline you feel is a sign that you care about your message and the audience, which can help channel that energy positively. Before your presentation, visualize a successful outcome. Picture yourself speaking confidently and receiving a positive response from the audience, which can help bolster your confidence.

Practice, Practice, Practice

The more thoroughly you prepare, the more confident you will feel. Familiarize yourself with your material and any technology you will be using. Role-play potential challenging situations with a friend or mentor, rehearsing how you would respond to disruptions or technical issues.

Handling difficult situations is an essential skill for any public speaker. By preparing for potential challenges such as technical difficulties and disruptive audience members, and by employing strategies to maintain composure, you can navigate these scenarios with confidence and professionalism. Remember, the way you respond to adversity not only affects your presentation but also sets an example for your audience. Embrace each challenge as an opportunity to grow and connect, and you will cultivate resilience that enhances your speaking journey.

Chapter 12- Taking the Stage

*Y*our voice matters. The world needs to hear your story.* As you stand on the precipice of opportunity, ready to share your unique message with the world, it's essential to cultivate a spirit of confidence and courage. Taking the stage, whether for a formal presentation, a community gathering, or a casual meeting, is not just about sharing information; it's about connecting with others and making an impact. To inspire your journey, we will motivate you to embrace speaking opportunities as we share testimonies from individuals who have overcome their fear of speaking. Their stories serve as a powerful reminder that with courage and practice, anyone can transform their anxiety into confidence and effectively share their message with the world. It's for you to *Take the Stage*!

Embracing Speaking Opportunities Confidently

Recognize the Value of Your Message:

Recognizing the value of your voice and message is a powerful realization that can transform how you approach communication and connection with others. Each person's life experiences are distinct, filled with lessons that can offer insights and perspectives different from anyone else's. When you acknowledge that your story is worth sharing, you empower yourself to engage authentically with others.

Understanding this value encourages you to reflect on your own experiences, challenges, and triumphs. It reminds you that your struggles and successes can serve as a beacon of hope or guidance for someone navigating similar paths. This intrinsic worth of your voice fosters confidence, allowing you to express yourself without fear of judgment. When you speak, you create an opportunity for dialogue, fostering understanding and empathy. You might be surprised at how your words can resonate deeply, triggering reflections and responses from those who hear them. Your message has the potential not only to inform but to inspire, comfort, or motivate others, creating a ripple effect of positive influence in their lives.

By embracing your unique voice, you not only honor your own journey but also contribute to a richer tapestry of shared human experience. This realization can transform public speaking from a daunting task into a fulfilling opportunity to connect, share, and inspire others who may be waiting for someone just like you to share what they need to hear.

Testimonies from Individuals Who Overcame the Fear of Public Speaking

Sarah's Story:

Sarah had always been terrified of public speaking. In school, she would avoid any opportunity to present in front of her classmates. After joining a local Toastmasters club, she started practicing in a supportive and nurturing environment. With each meeting, her confidence grew.

"The first time I took the stage, my heart raced. But as I spoke, I realized I was sharing something valuable. I felt liberated! Now, I love speaking and have even given a TEDx talk!" Sarah J.

Michael's Journey:

As an introverted professional, Michael often dreaded team meetings and would frequently remain silent, missing opportunities to share his ideas. Encouraged by a mentor, he began taking on small presentation roles in team settings, slowly building his confidence.

"I was always afraid of being judged. But when I started speaking up, I discovered my ideas were valued. Now, I confidently lead workshops in my company, and it's been incredibly rewarding." Michael F.

Lisa's Experience:

Lisa had experienced a traumatic speaking event during high school, which left her with a deep fear of public speaking. After attending a personal development seminar, she vowed to confront her fears. She began volunteering to speak at community events.

"The first few times were nerve-wracking, but each experience helped me heal and grow. Now, I facilitate community discussions, and I feel empowered to share my story and encourage others." Lisa R.

Taking the stage can feel intimidating, but it is also an opportunity for growth, connection, and impact. As you embrace speaking opportunities with confidence, remember the value of your message and the potential it has to resonate with others. The testimonies of those who have overcome their fears remind us that transformation is possible through persistence and self-belief. Let their journeys inspire you as you prepare to step onto the stage, knowing that your voice matters and that you have the power to make a meaningful difference in the lives of those who are privileged to hear you speak.

Chapter 13- Continuous Growth

The journey of becoming an effective communicator is ongoing; every experience is an opportunity to learn and grow. Public speaking is a skill that can be continually refined and enhanced. As you've taken significant steps toward overcoming fear and improving your speaking abilities, it's crucial not to become complacent. Lifelong learning and ongoing growth in your communication skills will not only keep you relevant but also empower you to become an even more effective speaker and leader. Exploring the importance of continual improvement in public speaking and providing valuable resources for your development is paramount. Let's begin!

The Importance of Lifelong Learning

The Ever-Evolving Landscape of Communication:

Communication styles, technologies, and audience expectations are constantly changing. To remain effective in your speaking endeavors, it's paramount to stay informed and adapt to new trends and practices. Embracing change and being open to new methods allows you to connect more effectively with diverse audiences.

Building on Your Foundation:

Each speaking engagement gives you valuable experience and insight. Reflecting on what went well and what could be improved will strengthen your abilities for future opportunities. Adopting a mindset that welcomes learning transforms challenges into growth opportunities, enhancing both your confidence and competence.

Networking and Learning from Others:

Engaging with fellow speakers and communicators offers fresh perspectives and diverse experiences. The relationships you build can lead to mentorship opportunities and collaborative learning. Additionally, actively participating in forums and discussions helps cultivate a supportive network that fosters personal growth and development.

Resources for Ongoing Development

Books on Public Speaking and Communication:

- *"Talk Like Ted" by Carmine Gallo*
  This book explores the techniques used by the most engaging TED speakers, providing readers with actionable tips to enhance their public speaking skills.[4]

- *"Dare to Lead" by Brené Brown*
  While focused on leadership, this book discusses the importance of vulnerability in communication, providing insights into authentic connection with audiences.[2]

- *"The Art of Public Speaking" by Dale Carnegie*
  A classic in the field, this book offers timeless principles and practical advice for effective public speaking.[3]

Online Courses:

The internet offers various courses on public speaking, communication, and presentation skills, often provided by reputable universities. This medium features a wide array of affordable courses tailored to specific areas of public speaking and communication techniques.

Speaking Groups and Clubs:

To find local meetup groups, search for public speaking or communication-focused groups in your area where members can practice together and share experiences. Many churches and community organizations offer speaking opportunities for their members, which can provide valuable practice while fostering personal growth.

Workshops and Conferences:

- Attend Speaking Workshops: Look for workshops organized by professional trainers that can provide hands-on experience and feedback.
- Conferences: Participate in industry-specific conferences that often include public speaking sessions, enhancing both knowledge and speaking skills in relevant contexts.

Continuing growth in speaking is a lifelong commitment that not only enhances your skills but also improves your overall effectiveness as a communicator. By embracing learning opportunities, seeking resources, and engaging in community support, you can refine your presentation skills and amplify your impact. Remember, every speaking opportunity presents a chance to learn, and through dedication to continuous improvement, you will thrive in sharing your message with confidence and purpose.

aspire to inspire

Chapter 14- Inspiring Others

Your journey of overcoming fear is not just for you; it has the power to inspire those around you. As you navigate the path of transforming fear into freedom, it's essential to recognize that your experiences can have a profound impact on the lives of others. When you bravely confront your fears and embrace opportunities for growth, you not only transform your own life but also inspire and empower those who witness your journey. Finally, we will explore how overcoming fear can positively affect those around you and discuss the importance of sharing your story to uplift others.

The Ripple Effect of Overcoming Fear

Modeling Resilience and Courage:

When you confront public speaking fears and succeed, you become a living testament to resilience. Your courage serves as a powerful example for others facing similar obstacles. People may feel encouraged to step out of their comfort zones upon witnessing your determination, realizing that they, too, can conquer their fears. Consider how many individuals have found motivation from public figures or leaders who openly share their struggles. By sharing your story, you can help others see that it's possible to overcome hurdles.

Creating a Supportive Environment:

Overcoming fear often requires fostering an environment of understanding and encouragement. As you grow in confidence, you can help cultivate a culture where vulnerability is respected and encourage others to share their fears. Your insecurity becomes inspiration!

This supportive environment can nurture stronger relationships within your community, leading to collaboration, trust, and mutual growth. Can you envision a mentoring relationship where your success encourages others to engage in public speaking or share their stories openly?

Encouraging the Pursuit of Passion:

By addressing your fears and showcasing your abilities, you inspire others to follow their passions and pursue their dreams. Your transformation can motivate those around you to take their first steps toward personal goals they've held back from achieving. People may realize they, too, have important messages to share and can begin working to develop their talents. Whether through informal conversations or formal workshops, sharing the journey encourages people to envision themselves overcoming their fears and succeeding.

Share Your Journey

The Power of Storytelling:

We have covered so much. Now it is activation time. Are you unsure of a speaking topic? Why not share your story? Your personal journey of overcoming fear is a powerful story that can resonate with others. Storytelling connects us and fosters empathy. By sharing your experiences, you create a platform for open dialogue about fears around public speaking. Consider writing a blog post, sharing it on social media, or speaking at a local event to inspire others who struggle with similar fears.

Empowering Others with Resources:

In your journey, you will have likely discovered useful strategies and resources for overcoming fear. Sharing these resources, such as books, workshops, or techniques, can provide direct assistance to others. Create a list of the top resources that helped you and encourage others to explore these options in their own journeys.

Creating Opportunities for Engagement:

Host workshops or discussion groups where individuals can share their fears and experiences in a safe and supportive space. Facilitating these environments allows for mutual support and growth. Encouraging dialogue about fears and challenges normalizes these feelings, making it easier for others to engage and seek help.

Becoming a Mentor

Offer your support to others who may be on the journey of overcoming fear themselves. As a mentor, you can guide them, providing encouragement and accountability. Share your insights in one-on-one settings, create leaderless discussion groups, or volunteer to assist in community organizations that focus on building confidence and skills in public speaking.

Your journey of overcoming fear in public speaking is an empowering story that has the potential to inspire and uplift those around you. By modeling resilience, creating a supportive atmosphere, and sharing your experiences, you help others recognize their capacity to face fears and pursue their passions. As you embrace your newfound freedom, remember that your story and actions can empower others, fostering a community of courageous individuals who are ready to share their voices and make a positive impact. Together, we can change lives and communities through the power of storytelling and shared experiences.

Conclusion

As we conclude our journey through Transforming Fear into Freedom: Your Guide to Confident Speaking, let us take a moment to recap the key themes and strategies we've explored together. We have examined the nature of fear, debunked myths surrounding public speaking, and emphasized the significance of preparation and practice. We discussed the vital role of understanding your audience, the art of storytelling, and the importance of maintaining composure during challenging situations. Each chapter has equipped you with practical techniques and insights that empower you to embrace public speaking with confidence and enthusiasm.

Transformation from fear to freedom is not merely a distant dream; it is a real possibility that anyone can achieve with commitment and consistent practice. The skills you've learned are not just tools for speaking; they are valuable life skills that will serve you well in every area of your personal and professional life. Remember that even the most accomplished speakers started as beginners, facing their fears and navigating their paths to success.

Now, I invite you to step into your newfound confidence and embrace your speaking journey. Each opportunity to speak is a chance to share your voice, connect with others, and make an impact. Challenge yourself to seek out speaking engagements, practice regularly, and continue to grow. Your unique perspective and story matter, and the world is waiting to hear what you have to say.

As you move forward, carry the lessons from this book with you, knowing that you have the power to overcome fear and shine brightly in every opportunity. Embrace the journey, celebrate your progress, and keep moving toward the freedom and fulfillment that comes from speaking with confidence. Together, let's transform fear into an empowering force for good, inspiring others as you boldly *Take the Stage*.

Thank you for joining me on this transformative journey. Here's to your continued growth and success as a confident speaker!

Notes

1. American Psychological Association. (n.d.). *Public speaking anxiety.* https://www.apa.org

2. Brown, B. (2018). *Dare to Lead: Brave Work. Tough conversations. Whole hearts.* Random House.

3. Carnegie, D. (2012). *The Art of Public Speaking (Updated Edition).* Simon & Schuster.

4. Gallo, C. (2014). *Talk Like TED: The 9 Public-Speaking Secrets of the World's Top Minds.* St. Martin's Press.

5. National Institute of Mental Health. (n.d.). *Anxiety disorders.* U.S. Department of Health and Human Services. https://www.nimh.nih.gov/health/topics/anxiety-disorders

6. University of California. (n.d.). *Fear of public speaking statistics.* https://www.universityofcalifornia.edu

Appendix

This appendix provides valuable tools and resources to support your journey in overcoming the fear of speaking and developing your skills as a confident communicator. Here, you will find additional self-assessment tools, goal-setting worksheets, and reflection exercises, as well as a resource list for further reading and training in public speaking.

FEAR QUESTIONNAIRE

Reflect on your fears related to public speaking using the following questions. Write down your answers to gain clarity on your triggers.

1 What specific situations cause you anxiety when speaking? (e.g., large audiences, unfamiliar settings)

2 How do you feel physically when you think of speaking in public? (e.g., sweaty palms, racing heart)?

3 What negative thoughts run through your mind before or during a speaking engagement?

4 Are there past experiences that contribute to your current fear of speaking? Describe them briefly.

REFLECTION TIME

Speaking Experiences
Instructions: Think of recent instances
where you had to speak publicly. Respond
to the following:

1 Describe the situation (e.g., audience, topic spoken).

2 How did you feel before, during, and after the experience?

3 What were the reactions of your audience?

4 What lessons did you learn from this experience?

GOAL SETTING

Instructions: Use this worksheet to establish specific and achievable goals for your public speaking development.

Goal:

Why It Matters:

Steps to Achieve This Goal:

Deadline for Achievement:

Reflection: What obstacles might I encounter, and how can I overcome them?

_____

_____

_____

_____

_____

_____

WEEKLY JOURNAL

Instructions: Each week, use this reflection journal to assess your progress and experiences.

1 What did I practice or learn this week?

2 How did I feel during my speaking opportunities?

3 What went well, and what can I improve?

4 How can I apply what I learned moving forward?

Resource List for Further Reading and Training on Public Speaking

Books:

1. Brown, B. (2018). *Dare to Lead: Brave Work. Tough conversations. Whole hearts.* Random House.

2. Carnegie, D. (2012). *The Art of Public Speaking (Updated Edition).* Simon & Schuster.

3. Gallo, C. (2014). *Talk Like TED: The 9 Public-Speaking Secrets of the World's Top Minds.* St. Martin's Press.

Online Courses:

- Coursera: Offers various public speaking courses from reputable institutions, which often include peer feedback. Coursera. (n.d.). *Coursera.* https://www.coursera.org

- Udemy: Features a range of affordable courses on public speaking techniques and communication skills. Udemy. (n.d.). *Udemy.* https://www.udemy.com

- Toastmasters International: Join a local chapter to practice speaking and receive constructive feedback in a supportive environment. Toastmasters International. (n.d.). *Toastmasters International.* https://www.toastmasters.org

Websites and Organizations:

SpeakerHub: A resource that connects speakers with opportunities and provides tips on public speaking. SpeakerHub. (n.d.). *Find and connect with public speakers and speaking opportunities.* https://speakerhub.com/

TED: Explore TED Talks for inspiration and learn from renowned speakers on effective communication. TED. (n.d.). *TED: Ideas worth spreading.* https://www.ted.com/

Podcasts:

"The Speaker Lab": Offers tips, strategies, and interviews with successful speakers. The Speaker Lab. (n.d.). *Learn how to grow your speaking business.* https://thespeakerlab.com/

Quick and Dirty Tips. (n.d.). *The Public Speaker: Public Speaking Tips and Speech Techniques.* https://www.quickanddirtytips.com/the-public-speaker/

This appendix serves as a supportive toolkit to help you continue your journey in overcoming the fear of public speaking. Remember, every step you take is part of the transformative journey toward thriving in speaking opportunities. Keep pushing forward!

About the Author

Dwayne is married to Esther Marcellus-Perry. He is a dedicated servant of Christ and passionate about empowering individuals to reach their full potential. With a heart rooted in love and a deep desire to see others thrive, he serves others out of an apostolic anointing. Driven by a genuine love for people, Dwayne seeks to uplift and inspire through coaching, mentoring, writings, teachings, and ministry.

Dwayne is a remarkable individual who has attained his Doctorate in Education and Ministry. His life's journey has been marked by excellence, service, education, and a deep commitment to empowering others. With a career spanning 13 years as a professional basketball player, Dwayne's passion for sports and his unwavering dedication to his craft have shaped him into the person he is today. Beyond his achievements on the court, Dwayne's true calling lies in his ability to serve others out of an apostolic anointing. Recognized as an anointed teacher, he possesses a unique gift for imparting wisdom and inspiring transformation in the lives of those he encounters. Through his teachings, Dwayne has touched countless hearts, helping individuals unlock their full potential and discover their purpose. As a coach, mentor, and developer of people, he has made it his mission to guide others on their journey toward personal and professional growth.

His commitment to nurturing talent and fostering a spirit of excellence has earned him the respect and admiration of those he has had the privilege to work with. Dwayne's ability to see the potential in others and empower them to reach new heights is a testament to his servant-hearted nature.

In addition to his athletic and teaching prowess, Dwayne is a sought-after speaker and motivator. His captivating presence and ability to connect with diverse audiences make him a powerful force for change. Through his engaging talks, he challenges individuals to overcome obstacles, embrace their unique gifts, and live a life of purpose and significance. His life experiences, both on and off the court, have shaped his character and fueled his passion for making a positive impact. His unwavering commitment to serving others, combined with his natural leadership abilities, have positioned him as a catalyst for transformation in the lives of many.

As you embark on this journey through the pages of this book, allow Dwayne's wisdom, insights, and experiences to inspire and empower you. His unique blend of athletic prowess, spiritual anointing, and dedication to developing people will undoubtedly leave a lasting impact on your life. Prepare to be challenged, motivated, and equipped as you delve into the transformative teachings of Dr. Dwayne C. Perry, a former professional basketball player, an anointed teacher, a coach, mentor, and a developer of people.

www.ingramcontent.com/pod-product-compliance
Lightning Source LLC
Chambersburg PA
CBHW071057090426
42737CB00013B/2365